Simply Science

MOVING ON LAND

Steve Way & Gerry Bailey

Illustrations: Steve Boulter & Xact Studio

Diagrams: Karen Radford

AUTHORS: GERRY BAILEY
STEVE WAY
EDITOR: FELICIA LAW
ILLUSTRATORS:
STEVE BOULTER
XACT STUDIO
DESIGN: FANNY MASTERS
RALPH PITCHFORD

ISBN 978-1-906292-15-7
Printed in China

PHOTO CREDITS:

p.5 PCL/Alamy
p.9 Dorling Kindersley Images.
p.12 Dorling Kindersley Images.
p.16 Piotr Przeszlo/Shutterstock Inc.
p.19 Sean Sexton/Corbis
p.21 Mike Butler/Shutterstock Inc.
p.23 Dorling Kindersley courtesy of the
National Motor Museum, Beaulieu.
p.24 (t) Daimler Chrysler AG; (b) The Car
Photo Library.
p.25 (t) Christophe Testi/Shutterstock Inc.
(m) Andres Rodriguez/Shutterstock Inc.
(b) The Motoring Picture Library.
p.27 Jolin/Shutterstock Inc.
p.28 NASA/Johnson Space Centre
p.29 NASA/JPL/Cornell University.

Cover
Oksanaperkins/Shutterstock

Simply Science

MOVING ON LAND

Contents

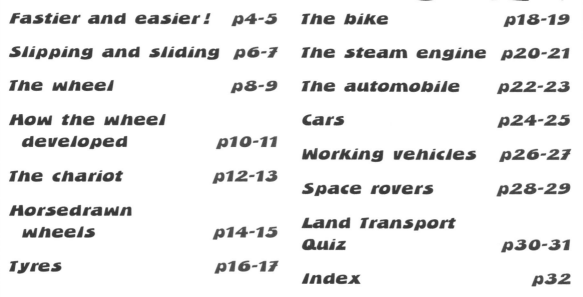

Faster and easier!

Ever since prehistoric times, many thousands of years ago, humans have needed to travel from place to place. As time went on, they also needed to go faster and to carry more and more goods with them. They must have been thrilled with the invention of the wheel! This really helped them!

But our ancient ancestors could never have imagined the different land vehicles we would create in the centuries that followed.

As you will find out from this book, land vehicles:

carry us across different kinds of land all across the globe,

carry our loads,

help us work, and

even explore the Moon!

Slipping and sliding

In some parts of the globe children believe that Santa Claus flies around the world on a sleigh pulled by flying reindeer. Santa is delivering presents to all the children who've been good.

It's a lovely idea and although some sleighs are indeed pulled by reindeer, none of them can fly – unfortunately. Sleighs are more often pulled by horses, oxen or dogs!

Sleighs

Sleighs use runners for sliding rather than wheels that roll. In fact, even though the sledge is an ancient invention, it's still the most efficient vehicle to use in thick snow! Many polar explorers used sleighs to pull their loads.

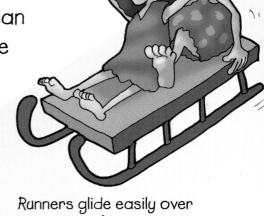

Runners glide easily over smooth surfaces such as snow, ice or grass.

Skis

Skis were originally used by people living in snowy regions who needed to travel over soft powdery snow or ice. Today, skiing is a popular form of sport at ski resorts all over the world.

At the start, skis were just flat boards. Later they curved upwards at the front to stop them digging into the snow. Many modern skis also curve inwards towards the middle, to make them easier to turn, and some are even curved upwards at the back as well as the front to allow the skier to go backwards and do all sorts of daring stunts!

Snowmobiles

Snowmobiles are an exciting, modern way of travelling about on snow. They are usually moved by one or two rubber belts that push against the snow, and steered by skis at the front of the vehicle. Snowmobiles are often used by reindeer herders instead of old-fashioned sleighs.

If they are driven fast enough, snowmobiles can even skim over water!

The wheel

A wheel is a round disc that can be made to spin across the ground. It can then be used to move any load placed on top of it.

Wheels are used to help move heavy weights. Many people believe that the wheel was the most important invention ever made because it made travel and transport easier.

It all looks so simple now!

Wheels that help move loads

1. Long ago, if you wanted to move a person, or a heavy load, you had to drag or push the load along the ground.

2. This meant using muscle power!

Friction

When moving objects touch, they rub against each other. This rubbing movement, which we call friction, causes moving objects to slow down. We see the effects of friction all around us. When you fall over and your elbow gets scraped, it is because of friction between your elbow and the floor.

These children are using friction to rub things smooth.

3. The idea for a wheel probably came to someone who used rolling logs to help move a load. Even so, this was still slow because the logs had to be moved from the back to the front as the load moved forward.

4. But the biggest problem of all was something we call friction. However hard you pushed and pulled, the rubbing force called friction would hold you back.

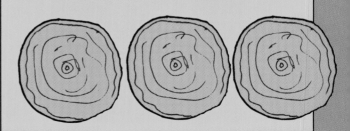

How the wheel developed

No-one really knows who invented the wheel. Many archeologists believe it was in use 8,000 years ago – that's long before the Ancient Greeks and Romans! The oldest wheel known was discovered in a part of Asia known as Sumeria.

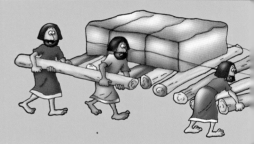

I wish this wasn't such hard work!

Runners and rollers

1. Long ago people put rollers under heavy objects so they could be moved more easily. The rollers had to be carried from the back to the front as the load moved forward.

2. Runners were placed under heavy loads. This made a kind of sledge so the load could be more easily dragged along. The sledge and the rollers were combined.

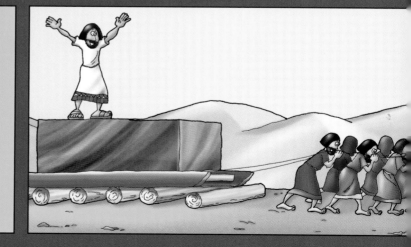

Horsepower

The speed at which a vehicle moves is often measured in horsepower. One horsepower is equal to a horse lifting a 75-kilogram load over a distance of 1 metre in just one second of time.

3. In time grooves were worn into the rim so the wood between the grooves was cut away. This made an axle joined to a wheel at both ends.

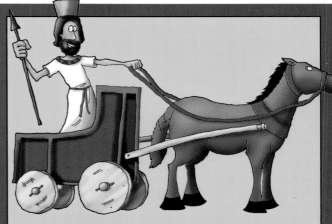

4. Then a hole was cut through the middle of the wheel and the wheel now spun round on the axle. As it spun, it carried a cart or fast-moving chariot, along with it.

The chariot

A chariot is a fast kind of cart. Carts were simple vehicles used for carrying loads. They had two or four wheels and were usually pulled along by cattle or horses. But chariots, had just two spoked wheels. They were light and easy to steer and mainly used in fighting battles.

Spoked wheels

The wheel was improved even more by the Egyptians. They made wheels with spokes for their chariots. Slim spokes made wheels much lighter.

Wheels with spokes

1. The first carts were heavy wooden vehicles. They were used by farmers to haul hay and vegetables and other heavy loads. But they weren't so good for carrying soldiers into battle. Strong armies needed something that was faster.

2. They needed something light and springy that would travel fast and turn corners easily.

3. The old carts needed some changes! The first things that were altered were the wheels. The old cart wheels were solid and heavy. Perhaps it would help, if the wheels were lighter?

4. So sections were cut out of the centre of the solid wheel.

5. Then things went further. If the wheels weren't solid at all but made from light spokes joined to the hub in the middle, they would be lighter still. And lighter wheels would be bouncy and move very fast too.

Horse-drawn wheels

Although modern cars known as 'people carriers' have only been around for a short while, vehicles have been used to carry people for thousands of years.

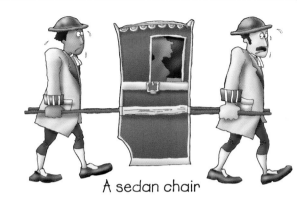
A sedan chair

In Roman times, when lots of well-built roads existed, many different kinds of vehicles pulled by animals were developed to use on them. Later on came heavy carriages and wagons.

Then, early in the 17th century in Sedan in France, the first real people carrier was used! The passenger sat on a chair inside and two people carried the sedan chair using handles.

A rickshaw is a kind of chair pulled along on wheels.

A rickshaw

Eventually, coaches were also developed and used for transporting people around towns. While stagecoaches were used for travelling the country from town to town.

A stagecoach

Early in the 19th century, a horse-drawn omnibus was used in Paris to carry people round the city. Steam-driven buses soon followed.

A horse-drawn omnibus

Later, taxis known as hansom cabs, became very popular for moving around the city. These carriages had two large wheels and could carry two passengers.

A hansom cab

Tyres

Ever since the car was invented, a band of rubber or rubber-like material has covered the rim of each wheel. It's called a tyre and it was designed to make travel by car more comfortable and safer.

Tread describes the marked pattern cut into the rubber tyre to help it grip the road.

A smooth ride

1. Early cars were very uncomfortable to ride in. The tyres had a knobbly surface, and were solid, making the car difficult to control.

2. Pneumatic tyres were invented. These were rubber tyres with inner tubes filled with air. The air pressure had to be high, which meant that they punctured easily.

3. Tyres with grooves cut into the rubber, called treads, gave the car a better grip on the road.

Wire tyres

Very special tyres had to be used for the lunar roving vehicle that explored the Moon. There is no air on the Moon that could be pumped into its tyres, so the rover had special lightweight metal tyres, made out of woven piano wire, instead!

4. Spare tyres were added so drivers could get going again if they got a puncture.

5. It wasn't until World War II that strong, wide tyres without inner tubes were developed. These tyres made an air-tight seal with the wheel hub.

6. Radial tyres are fitted to modern cars. These are made with layers of strong wire cords running diagonally around the inside of the tyre. They are fast and safe and have good grip.

1. Not long ago most people had to get around by walking. So they usually didn't travel too far from home!

2. Of course, wealthier people could ride a horse or take a stagecoach. But for most people, walking was the only cheap and easy way to travel.

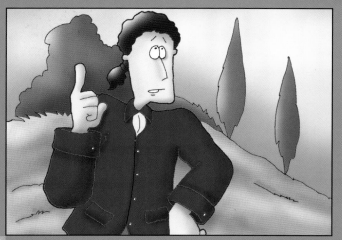

3. Surely there was a way in which a person could be carried along on wheels? People were strong enough to push wheels round, but could they do this and be carried quickly across the ground?

4. At last, the bicycle was invented. Two wheels were joined together by an axle and fixed to a frame. Pedals were attached to the axle by a chain and as the rider's feet turned the pedals, the wheels turned too. At the same time, the rider could perch above the wheels and steer with handlebars.

The bike

A bike, or bicycle, is a vehicle that has two wheels. It is powered by the rider.

One wheel is fixed behind the other and both are held in place by a frame.

Early models

The first pedal bike was called a velocipede, or 'boneshaker', because it had no springs and was a bumpy ride. The penny-farthing came later. It had one enormous wheel at the front and a tiny one at the rear.

Finally the 'safety bicycle' was invented that had two wheels of equal size and was much easier to ride. This is the kind of bike we ride today.

The steam locomotive

A steam locomotive is a vehicle that is powered by a steam engine. It is used to pull carriages or trucks along iron rails.

There's got to be a better way!

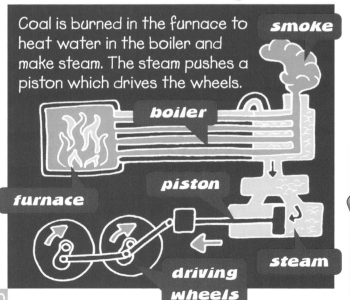

Coal is burned in the furnace to heat water in the boiler and make steam. The steam pushes a piston which drives the wheels.

smoke

boiler

piston

furnace

steam

driving wheels

Steam that turns wheels

1. Up to the 1800s, many factory owners had to use a horse-drawn cart to carry their goods from place to place.

2. Then an inventor called Richard Trevithick had the brilliant idea of building a pulling machine.

3. Trevithick invented a steam-powered engine. Steam from the steam engine pushes against a piston in a cylinder at the side of the locomotive. The piston then pushes the big driving wheels.

I'll burn coal to heat water and make steam.

4. As the piston moves backwards and forwards in the cylinder, it turns the wheels.

Railways

Steam locomotives ran on iron rails, which made the ride smooth and fast. Soon a network of powerful steam locomotives criss-crossed every major country of the world, carrying goods and people, and connecting cities everywhere.

An old steam locomotive from the American 'Wild West'. The railways helped open up the west of America to settlers.

The automobile

An automobile, or motor car, is a road vehicle that is usually powered by an engine known as the 'internal combustion engine'.

Hello. I'm Karl Benz – the man who invented the automobile.

Internal combustion engine

Inside an internal combustion engine, a moving piston draws in air and helps to squeeze it. The squeezed air gets very hot. A jet of petrol is mixed with the hot air and explodes. This sudden power pushes the piston down which turns a crankshaft. This happens over and over again very fast, driving the car forward.

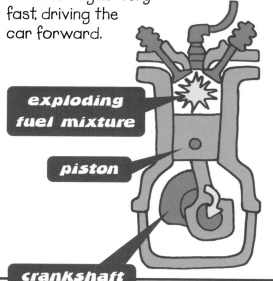

exploding fuel mixture

piston

crankshaft

1. A German inventor called Karl Benz was interested in developing the automobile as a new way of transport. So he set to work. He built an internal combustion engine that could be used in a traditional carriage. He fitted the engine in the back and attached it to the rear wheels.

Benz's car

Benz built his little three-wheeled car in 1885 and sold his first one two years later. He completed production of a four-wheeled model in 1893, and the Mercedes-Benz company started by the inventor, was the world's largest manufacturer of automobiles by 1900.

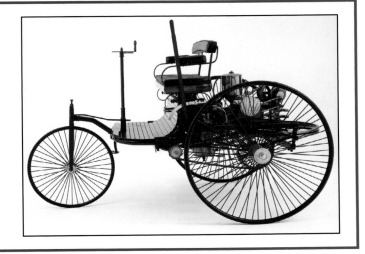

2. The engine had pistons inside cylinders. When petrol and air were ignited by a spark, the pistons pushed down and turned a crankshaft. The shaft was attached to the two back wheels by a chain.

3. The front wheel was fitted with a handle so that the car could be steered.

Cars

The design of cars has changed a lot since Karl Benz made his three-wheeled car. Early car makers like Benz and Gottlieb Daimler based their designs on vehicles they were familiar with – horse-drawn carriages. That's why their cars were sometimes called 'horseless carriages'!

Early car designs were sometimes called three-box designs. They had a 'box' for the engine, one to carry the passengers and one for the luggage. Unfortunately, boxes aren't the sort of shape that moves easily through the air. They're not streamlined.

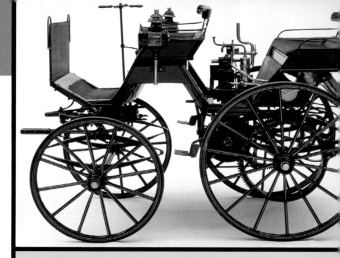

The first Daimler car adapted from a horse-drawn carriage.

Enclosed cars

Early cars were open-topped and uncomfortable to ride in. So makers began designing cars with the engine at the front and a closed body behind to keep passengers warm and dry.

A 1934 Austin Seven.

BYL 460

Mass production

Henry Ford developed a way of making hundreds of cars at a time by putting them together piece by piece on conveyor belts in a huge factory. The parts were all a standard size, so cars all looked the same but became much cheaper. More and more people could afford to buy them.

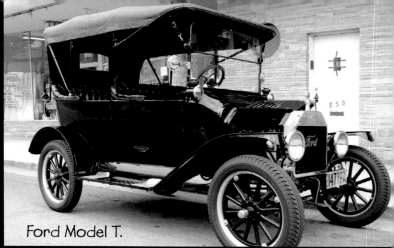

Ford Model T.

Ferrari 348.

Aerodynamics

Designers knew they had to make their cars more streamlined, or aerodynamic, so they would move faster. They shaved off the square edges and made cars more rounded, slimmer, and more sporty to look at.

Hybrids

The less aerodynamic a car is, the more fuel it needs to go quickly. And the more fuel it uses, the more it pollutes the air. Hybrid cars use a mix of petrol and electricity for power. But they are also shaped to pass easily through the air and use even less polluting fuel.

Toyota Prius.

Working vehicles

Strong, tough machines are needed to plough the land and haul crops and farm machinery from place to place. These farm machines need to travel on rough and muddy land without getting stuck.

The plough

Animal-drawn ploughs have been used to turn the soil for thousands of years.

Steam tractor

The first tractor powered by steam arrived in the 1770s. The engine and boiler were mounted above the front wheel. The tractor was steered using a hand lever. It could heave an incredible 8 tonnes of weight but at a snail-like speed of just 12 kilometres an hour!

Army wheels

In the 1900s, an American tractor company, Holt, developed a kind of wheel known as a caterpillar track, to help their heavy tractors move on soft ground without sinking. These were the same caterpillar tracks that were later used on heavy army tanks.

Tractors

Tractors must be able to move easily over muddy soil without sinking or slipping. They have front and back wheels that are much closer together than in a car and the rear wheels are very large. This keeps the tractor firmly on the ground.

I wish we'd had one of those in my day

Space rovers

Land vehicles have even been put to work in space. The space buggy allowed astronauts to move about, exploring the Moon's surface further and more safely than they could have done on foot.

The solar-powered rovers, Spirit and Opportunity, have managed to travel even further on Mars than we expected. They have helped us learn so much more about our nearest neighbour. It's likely that more rovers will be sent to Mars in the near future.

Lunar Rover

Three lunar roving vehicles were driven on the Moon on three missions. Each made three journeys.

Mars Exploration Rover

NASA's long-lived Mars Exploration Rover, Spirit, has been exploring the surface of Mars since January 2004 and sending back lots of pictures.

It's pretty bumpy on Mars

Land Transport Quiz

1. What do we call the 'rubbing' force that slows things down?

_____

2. Where was the oldest known wheel discovered?

_____

3. What kind of vehicle was a hansom cab?

_____

4. What was missing from a velocipede, which meant it was called a 'boneshaker'?

_____

5. Steam engines were the idea of which inventor?

6. Who had the idea of putting spokes on wheels to make them lighter?

_____

7. What piece of furniture was a sedan chair modelled on?

_____

8. What were the lightweight metal tyres of the lunar roving vehicle made from?

_____

9. Who built the first car?

_____

10. Who developed the mass production of cars?

_____

1. Friction 2. Sumeria, Asia 3. A taxi 4. Springs! 5. Richard Trevithick
6. The Egyptians 7. France 8. Piano Wire 9. Karl Benz 10. Henry Ford

31

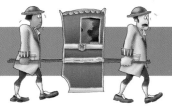

Index